THE BENJAMIN F. FAIRLESS
MEMORIAL LECTURES

An internationally known figure from the worlds of business, government, or education is invited each year to present three lectures at Carnegie-Mellon University under the auspices of its Graduate School of Industrial Administration.

In general, the lectures will be concerned with some aspects of business or public administration; the relationships between business and government, management and labor; or a subject related to the themes of preserving economic freedom, human liberty, and the strengthening of individual enterprise—all of which were matters of deep concern to Mr. Fairless throughout his career.

Mr. Fairless was president of United States Steel Corporation for fifteen years, and chairman of the board from 1952 until his retirement in 1955. A friend of Carnegie-Mellon University for many years, he served on the board of trustees from 1952 until his death. In 1959 he was named honorary chairman of the board.

Eli Goldston, President of Eastern Gas and Fuel Associates, is equally at home in both industrial and academic circles in the United States, England, Europe and Japan.

Referring to his efforts for the past decade to make an international diversified energy firm not only highly profitable but also socially progressive, Fortune Magazine described him as "the man who taught a corporate elephant to dance." He serves as a director of many businesses including Algonquin Gas Transmission Company, The First National Bank of Boston, John Hancock Mutual Life Insurance Company, Arthur D. Little, Inc., and Raytheon Company.

In addition to holding four earned academic degrees from Harvard University (economics, law and business management), Mr. Goldston has been awarded honorary degrees by Babson College, Bates College and Boston College. He serves on visiting committees at Harvard University, Massachusetts Institute of Technology and Carnegie-Mellon University, and is a director of the National Bureau of Economic Research and a member of the Council of the American Academy of Arts and Sciences.

For several years he has been on the faculty of the Salzburg Seminars in American Studies. Presently Mr. Goldston is on sabbatical from his business duties and is spending the first half of 1972 as Visiting Fellow at the London Graduate School of Business Studies where he is both studying and teaching the subjects of Advanced Asset Management and Corporate Social Responsibility.

He brings to the 1971 Benjamin F. Fairless Memorial Lectures on the role of the public corporation in a modern industrial democracy an unusual combination of experience in law, industry and academia.

1971 BENJAMIN F. FAIRLESS MEMORIAL LECTURES

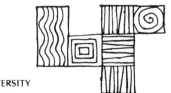

1971 CARNEGIE-MELLON UNIVERSITY

Library of Congress Catalog Card Number 72-75528
ISBN Number 0-231-03675-2

The Quantification of Concern
Some Aspects of Social Accounting

Eli Goldston

The Benjamin F. Fairless Memorial Lectures endowment fund has been established at Carnegie-Mellon University to support an annual series of lectures. An internationally known figure from the worlds of business, government, or education is invited each year to present three lectures at Carnegie-Mellon under the auspices of its Graduate School of Industrial Administration. In general, the lectures will be concerned with some aspects of business or public administration; the relationships between business and government, management and labor; or a subject related to the themes of preserving economic freedom, human liberty, and the strengthening of individual enterprise—all of which were matters of deep concern to Mr. Fairless throughout his career.

Mr. Fairless was president of United States Steel Corporation for fifteen years, and chairman of the board from 1952 until his retirement in 1955. A friend of Carnegie-Mellon University for many years, he served on the board of trustees from 1952 until his death. In 1959 he was named honorary chairman of the board. He was also a leader and co-chairman of Carnegie-Mellon's first development program, from its beginning in 1957.

five

1971

Eli Goldston, President of Eastern Gas and Fuel Associates, is equally at home in both industrial and academic circles in the United States, England, Europe and Japan.

Referring to his efforts for the past decade to make an international diversified energy firm not only highly profitable but also socially progressive, Fortune Magazine described him as "the man who taught a corporate elephant to dance." He serves as a director of many businesses including Algonquin Gas Transmission Company, The First National Bank of Boston, John Hancock Mutual Life Insurance Company, Arthur D. Little, Inc., and Raytheon Company.

In addition to holding four earned academic degrees from Harvard University (economics, law and business management), Mr. Goldston has been awarded honorary degrees by Babson College, Bates College and Boston College. He serves on visiting committees at Harvard University, Massachusetts Institute of Technology and Carnegie-Mellon University, and is a director of the National Bureau of Economic Research and a member of the Council of the American Academy of Arts and Sciences.

For several years he has been on the faculty of the Salzburg Seminars in American Studies. Presently Mr. Goldston is on sabbatical from his business duties and is spending the first half of 1972 as Visiting Fellow at the London Graduate School of Business Studies where he is both studying and teaching the subjects of Advanced Asset Management and Corporate Social Responsibility.

He brings to the 1971 Benjamin F. Fairless Memorial Lectures on the role of the public corporation in a modern industrial democracy an unusual combination of experience in law, industry and academia.

Getting and spending lays waste late and soon, not only our powers, as William Wordsworth has suggested, but also—for the active business manager—his hours. These essays under the constraints of available time therefore reflect modest research in the relevant scholarly literature and light editing of the taped lectures. Consequently the reader should regard this book as a view of contemporary ocean life by an articulate fish rather than as the findings of a research team of professional ichthyologists.

Numerous people helped me prepare the lectures. Dean Cyert of Carnegie-Mellon Graduate School of Industrial Administration reviewed my first drafts and made several seminal suggestions. My business colleagues, primarily Messrs. Ingram, Leslie, Thompson and Weinig, cautioned and corrected. Finally my family, Elaine, Dian, Bob and Robbie, encouraged and edited. Ultimately, however, the Spanish verse holds true:

"Advice pours down from the stadium full,
But only the matador faces the bull."

Though these ideas may be less than novel and scanty of proof, they do reflect how the United States business scene appeared to one deeply involved and concerned observer in late 1971. Indeed, I have become sufficiently concerned to seek sabbatical leave from my business duties and am now pursuing farther the problems of quantifying social concerns as Visiting Fellow at the London Graduate School of Business Studies.

Eli Goldston
London, February 7, 1972

eleven

I. Social Indicators
Some National Goals
Beyond Greater GNP

I. Social Indicators
Some National Goals Beyond Greater GNP

There is a certain rhythm that you sense in our company name as some people pronounce it. You may have noticed that Professor Meltzer in introducing me emphasized the second word in "Eastern *Gas* and Fuel Associates." When I last talked to a campus audience a suggestion was made that we change that second word in our company name to "Eastern *Grass* and Fuel Associates." On that occasion I was introduced as a fellow who, if he would only do this, might be able to offer the public a much more entertaining trip than walking a mile for a Camel. At the time I was a bit startled by this introduction, but I suppose that one of the problems for those of us who are outside the campus is to get some sense of the changing values that exist on the campus and that sooner or later will exist in the outside world, including the business world.

When you discuss a business topic at Carnegie-Mellon University, you tend toward exploratory surgery, using the keen scalpel of higher mathematics. The Graduate School of Industrial Administration offers help to the struggling businessman in such articles as "Co-efficient Estimation in Quadratic Programming Models" and "Linear Programming in Optimal Bank Asset Management Decisions." But at Carnegie-Mellon in exploring an economic topic, you also tend to strive for illumination from the behavioral sciences, using tools that have been blunted by trying them out in the real world. After all, Dean Richard M. Cyert and Associate Dean Herbert A. Simon of the Carnegie-Mellon Business School have explored how managers of corporations actually make decisions in the business firm. They have created what is known as the behavioral theory of the firm and are significantly supplementing the traditional economic theory that most of us learned.

It is a quite similar conflict between the surgical precision of statistics and the rich uncertainty of wise decision-making that we'll try to explore in these Fairless Memorial Lectures—the conflict between the descriptive "is" and the normative "should be." The conflict is suggested in the general title of the lecture series: "The Quantification of Concern."

In the first lecture, we will discuss how changes in our national goals have made somewhat obsolete the traditional measure of national welfare—Gross National Product (perhaps better known by its abbreviation "GNP"). Throughout the lectures, there will be four recurring principles or ideas:

The first is that our priorities have been changing with some rapidity. Many of our political, economic and commercial measures of progress have become obsolescent. We need a new kind of social accounting that goes beyond GNP for the nation and goes beyond net profit for the firm.

Second, while we think of our current economic and accounting measures of GNP and net profit as very precise, when you really get into the nitty gritty of how they are put together, their certainty is delusive.

Third, many proposed imprecise measures of social accounting can be sufficiently accurate to be instructive. They are not hopelessly less accurate than GNP or net profit, and so they can be quite useful, even though they lack precision, for many purposes for which we can not use GNP and net profit.

And finally, while our efforts to calibrate our concerns by social accounting will reflect this new sense of priorities, without personal observation in the field and a weighting of the figures that we create with moral concerns, social accounting itself becomes only a new numbers game.

Let me illustrate this fourth point: That what we measure provides an insight into what kind of a person—or a firm—or a nation—we are. After all, people naturally keep track of the things that are most important to them. People on a diet step on every scale they pass. Misers keep constant track of their net worth. Even the most absent-minded of people seldom forget their own birthdays. Ralph Waldo Emerson once wrote "A man's library is a sort of harem, and tender readers have great prudency in showing their books to a stranger." It has also been suggested that you could learn a great deal about the state of mind of a nation by analyzing the circulation of its library books. But it isn't only in the books of literature in a library, but in the books of account you find in the national budget or in the ledgers of the business firm, that we reveal some of the goals and the priorities of the society, and of a company. The things we measure, how we measure them, the form in which we record and analyze the data, and to whom we disclose it, not only tell much about us but are also likely to have a considerable effect on the way we act.

To expand on Ralph Waldo Emerson's thought that a library is sort of a harem that reveals its owner's mind, let us recall the story of the Turkish Sultan, who was asked, "How many wives and how many children do you have?" He replied, "I have 35 wives, 17 of them are brunettes, 6 of them blondes, 4 red heads and 8 have grey hair. Of the 8 with grey hair, 2 originally were brunettes, 5 originally were blondes, and 1 originally was a red head. As for children, I really don't know, but there are a lot of them around. Some have gone abroad. Some are boys and some are girls, but I really don't bother trying to keep track of the children except for my eldest son who will succeed me. He's 6'2" tall and a student at Oxford University studying history with a minor in mathematics. His grades are excellent; he plays varsity rugby."

From that bit of accounting summarized in Figure I, you can learn quite a bit about the Sultan. You learn that he cares about the wives but only about the eldest child. He is an aesthete with an eye for hair color by which he classifies the ladies. But if you were to press him for more information about the wives, you might find that he doesn't know their ages, their nationalities, their religion, their weight, their height or most anything else about them except that 4 had won the Cordon Bleu in cooking, 19 more were quite good cooks and 7 couldn't cook at all. This suggests that the Sultan is a gourmet as well as an aesthete. One can't help wondering—particularly under the higher mathematics influence of Carnegie-Mellon—whether a matrix analysis of the available data might be extremely informative, such as Figure II.

On the basis of this data, if a young Turkish brunette wanted to prepare herself, to become a member of the Sultan's harem, she would, I think, conclude she should either learn how to cook, or if she has no talent in the kitchen, she had better dye her hair blonde or red. It would also appear that to remain

Figure I – *The Sultan's Wives–Blonde, Brunette, Redhead?*

seventeen

in the harem as a grey haired matron, any former brunette had better win the Cordon Bleu, since the matrix analysis indicates that the Sultan offers long-term housing for the elderly only to those who are originally blondes or red heads, or else, to brunettes who have won the Cordon Bleu.

Now the student of statistics will raise other issues. The distribution suggests there may be a lack of non-brunette cooks in the general population for reasons not very apparent, or it may indicate some peculiar reluctance of the Sultan to employ good blonde and red headed cooks. We need a general census of Turkey not just a tabulation of the harem for complete and rigorous statistical analysis! Of course the eager student of higher statistics would also have us press the Sultan—"give us heights, weights, I.Q.'s, blood pressures." He would have us make a matrix of much higher order—perhaps at Carnegie-Mellon we should try multiple curvilinear regression analysis. But the specialist can so expand his data base and so refine his tools of analysis that he misses the richness and illogic of real life and pulls conclusions out of his data that are sports or spurious correlations. He can devote himself to trying to answer with precision questions that do not need precise answers or that even cannot have precise answers.

It is true that Elizabeth Barrett Browning said: "How do I love thee? Let me *count* the ways." This suggests that careful calibration of all sorts of additional harem data might reveal all sorts of insights beyond our rough matrix. But remember that Browning's message was "Let *me*" (not some expert at statistical analysis)—but "Let *me* count the ways." To a behavioral analyst this should suggest that the things the Sultan and the poetess count are the things that enter their own conscious processes of decision.

We have to be careful, on the other hand, of the hidden assumption and the unconscious processes of decision. Often our decisions are really dictated not by fact and by logic, but by what we assume and express only if the right button is pushed; only if the right question is asked. All the analysis of the data in Figures I and II won't reveal why the Sultan always had 35 wives—never 1 more, never 1 less. What we need to know is that his father and his grandfather each had

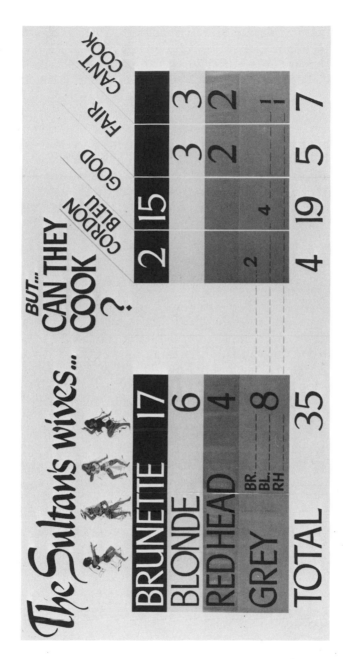

Figure II – *The Sultan's Wives–Can They Cook?*

35 wives and so the Sultan assumed—just as someone in America might assume that monogamy is a universal practice—that for the Sultan 35 was the obviously appropriate number. We also should consider the possibility of unconscious decisions not to make measurements. Suppose all 35 of our ladies have long noses and flat ears and thus look just like the Sultan's childhood sweetheart who jilted him. If you query him about this directly, he might say it is nonsense. But to what degree do we refuse to calibrate goals which we do not want to see that we are pursuing, or that we do not want to see that we have neglected? Remember that in another sonnet Elizabeth Barrett Browning pleaded against the calibration of concern, saying:

"If thou must love me, let it be for naught
Except for love's sake only.
Do not say, 'I love her (A) for her smile—(B) for her look—(C) for her way of speaking gently— or (D) for a trick of thought that falls in well with mine.'"

But what, you may ask, have the whims of a Sultan and the ambiguities of a poetess to do with the accounting of modern industrial nations and modern large corporations? What I have tried to emphasize in this way is that we measure what we feel is important to us; and I would suggest that the things that are important to us as an industrial nation have begun to change. Now that modern governments have come to assume that they can successfully intervene in almost any social problem of their populations and now that the public has come to regard large corporations as one of the major tools available to the government to solve these problems, the familiar measures of progress of our recent past—GNP for the country and net profit for the corporation—though they will continue to be fundamentally important, can no longer be the exclusive indicators of accomplishment.

The proposed substitutes for GNP and net profit, however, too often are used as cliches rather than as calibrations. We need to define more clearly some of our currently popular phrases: social responsibility, social accounting, social indicators and social audit.

The belief that maximizing profit has been the primary motive of the business firm and that this motive no longer fits society's expectation of the firm has led to the phrase "social responsibility" as some sort of new motive that will affect corporate decision makers—sometimes, but by no means always, in conflict with profit. "Social accounting" is the yet-to-be defined set of books to replace GNP for government and net profit for business, as a measure of the degree to which government improves the quality of life (and for poor people this may perhaps merely be an increase in quantity) and the degree to which business firms meet their social responsibility. There is no consensus on how to distill social accounts into some sort of a net figure comparable to GNP or net profit—a single figure that sums it all up. So we have developed the concept of "social indicators," that is separate sets of discrete statistics which, without being aggregated, provide a sort of a profile of our social welfare. One of these might be total days of illness-free life for the average citizen. Others might be the frequency of industrial accidents or the degree of air-pollution. But the methodology and even the meaning of much of this data has yet to be refined. Does an increase in hospital days reflect a terrible increase in environmental pollution or does it reflect the fact that with higher income and more hospitals it is possible to take better care of your population? In part because in any new area of statistics it becomes very easy for the figures to lie and the liars to figure, a "social audit" has been proposed where some outside entity tries to check whether statistics have been accurately brought together and if they really mean what it is claimed they do. When you struggle with these fuzzy concepts, you feel as if you were watching a cross-eyed discus thrower. You are doubtful that his performance is going to set any world record, but it certainly will keep the audience alert.

It is difficult to remember that until recently a growing GNP had a genuine popular appeal and was almost universally regarded as an indication of improved public welfare. In the Kennedy campaign for the presidency an important promise was: "He'll get the country moving. We've got to get the GNP crawling up again." Nations during post-World War II years have measured their progress by the yardstick of GNP and compared their progress by matching their GNP growth rates like youngsters standing back to back to see who is growing taller.

In order to understand how we developed this infatuation with GNP it is necessary to turn to a bit of history. Back in World War I, Bernard Baruch's War Production Board realized that the efforts to increase the output of war materials was hampered by our very sketchy knowledge of the size and the nature of our national industrial income. In 1920, after the war, the National Bureau of Economic Research was established as a private statistical research organization to gather together quantitive economic information in order to understand better the industrial society in which we were living. Building on studies of national income and national product in 17th and 18th century England, the National Bureau during the 1920's, largely guided by Simon Kuznets, who recently won the Nobel prize in economics, developed a whole system of accounts by which we could better understand the working of our economy.

Although by 1930 our statistics had been greatly improved, we had entered a critical period in the history of economic ideas much like the present crisis in our economic theory, in that the then popular interpretive theories of economics could not explain the then current social conditions and failed to offer solutions to the social problems. In the 1930 depression there were 16,000,000 unemployed Americans who obviously were not all lazy and who obviously were not all dodging an opportunity to get a job. This involuntary unemployment was inconsistent with the then current classical economics. To a society which measured its success by employment and by per capita income, the depression spelled failure.

An international debate developed on the question of how to cure the depression. This in turn created the need for more comprehensive national income information and theory. On the one hand Simon Kuznets at the National Bureau sharpened and developed his statistical tools, and on the other hand, John Maynard Keynes in England, using the Kuznets statistical researches as a foundation, propounded an entirely new economic theory that offered liberal democratic governments the hope that cyclical and secular stagnation could be prevented by astute government economic policy. But use of this policy required that the newly emerging field of national income measurement be developed into a broader system of national income accounting. By the late 30's, the National Bureau of Economic Research had its work taken over by the Department of Commerce, and we began to publish an official current estimate of national income. During World War II, the accounts were further refined to help control wartime output and inflation. Shortly after the war, the official concept of GNP, as we now know it, was born.

The National Economic Accounts which we popularly know as GNP, aim to measure the value of goods and services bought and sold in the market place. It is important to recognize what we are actually trying to measure with GNP as opposed to what we sometimes think it represents. It is the value of goods and services bought and sold in the market place. We have become accustomed, since the Council of Economic Advisors was established, to the idea of combining the theory of Keynes and the accounts of Kuznets to produce an official federal economic policy which expects the federal government to do things to produce full employment and growth in individual material well being. During the 1950's and the early 1960's, a rise in GNP, and more importantly, a rise in the rate of rise in GNP, had been almost universally regarded as objective proof of improved national welfare.

In order to understand what is happening to our attitude toward GNP and what is happening to the world of economics, it is useful to think of economic matters in the context of the general history of ideas. I should like to suggest that the succession of one orthodox majority school of economics by another can be compared with Thomas S. Kuhn's description of scientific revolutions. Such a comparison is useful because so many of us willingly accept new science and new technology but resist new economics and new politics, perhaps because we regard the latter two as threats to our personal values and status. We do not care to recognize our long-held economic values or inherited social beliefs as assumptions or tentative hypotheses rather than as established truths.

twenty-three

Kuhn has shown that the history of scientific revolutions is a repeated story of the overthrow of old accepted ideas by new ones which explain new and apparently incomprehensible data that has accumulated. Eventually the new ideas become the entrenched orthodoxy, are found incapable of explaining new data or solving new problems, and are themselves overthrown. Thus, as data accumulated inconsistent with the hypothesis that the sun revolved around the earth, Ptolemy's astronomy was replaced by the new ideas of Copernicus who better explained the data by a sun-centered (heliocentric) theory. The more rapidly field instruments (such as telescopes in Copernicus' case) are developed, the more rapidly anomalous data accumulates, and the more rapidly orthodox ideas have to be overthrown.

To further confuse us, however, frequently at the very time when anomalous material is accumulating to challenge the orthodoxy, a good deal of material is also developing to confirm the orthodoxy. Then the attack is often met by a rather violent counter-attack which is usually more violent in the social than in a technical field. After all, the only vested interests initially challenged by new scientific ideas are entrenched schools of thought, not entrenched positions in the social order. For such reasons, the Keynesian Revolution in economic thought became a public and political issue in a way that scientific revolutions have not been since the decline of the Church-State when religion and science were intertwined. Keynes has only recently become acceptable to conservative men like President Richard Nixon who, no doubt, never felt emotionally challenged at the start by the new ideas of Albert Einstein, which represented a similar form of revolution in intellectual thought.

Just as the effort of John Maynard Keynes to link growing economic knowledge to public policy forced great changes in what and how we sought to measure during the 1920's, 30's, 40's, and 50's, the effect of a trilogy of books on economics during the 1960's by John Kenneth Galbraith started a new revolution in economic thought, which is presently forcing us to a new evaluation of our national techniques of measurement. This new national debate about goals and priorities has raised the question about whether we are measuring the right things. We have begun talking about the "quality" rather than the "quantity" of life, by which we seem to mean such disparate efforts as assimilating minority groups into our social system, improving education, raising industrial health, enlarging medical care, improving appliance service, achieving truth in advertising, cultural enrichment, protection of the environment, conservation of resources, and almost anything else you can think of. GNP is keenly denounced as simply a measure of materialism by critics who do not really understand what it is or the purpose for which it is intended to be used. Others profess indeed to find a decline in social welfare which proceeds inversely with a rise in GNP—which they translate as "Grossest National Product" or "Gross National Pollution."

Much as it happened in the 1930's, we currently are dissatisfied with the ability of our economic theory to come up with solutions to the major social issues of our time. It is as if the Sultan were told to throw out all of his data on cooking and hair color and told he should keep track of his wives in the terms of days spent helping at day care centers and hours spent learning how to prepare organic meals, even weeks spent in organizing women's liberation movements. Perhaps such changes will come, but as is true of scientific revolutions, changes in our social and economic behavior will have to develop first from a clear understanding of the limits of what we already have. It is important, therefore, to understand what our GNP is and to plan our new measures with an eye to the difficulties of using them.

Finally, it is most important to recognize that while old orthodoxies may be insufficient to solve all the new problems, they may still retain a substantial value. The Ptolemaic system of astronomy, which assumed that the sun revolves around the earth, is actually still used today for a good many rough engineering approximations. The navigator of an ocean vessel still navigates on an underlying assumption that stars revolve around the earth; but the navigator of a space ship has to use post-Copernican astronomy. Keynesian economics has taught us how to meet mass unemployment and major depression. But although it does not offer solutions for some of the currently popular problems, it has left us free to contend with these remaining ills of a generally affluent society. We must constantly remember as we move beyond Keynes and Kuznets, that reducing unemployment a few percentage points by Keynesian economics probably produces a much more massive social gain than most of the currently popular proposals for social reform that still remain on our agenda.

There is an extensive scholarly bookshelf on the technical issues of producing GNP figures. These largely go to questions of mechanical detail rather than to the broader question of whether we are measuring the right thing and using the resulting figures for the right purposes—whether GNP can tell us anything about the quality as well as the quantities of life.

There are two ways of approaching this issue of measuring the quality of life. One is to take the existing GNP statistical system and try to adjust it so that we can measure not only economic production but social welfare—some sort of GNH or "Gross National Happiness." The second way is to try to set up a series of independent social accounts that supposedly will better measure progress in areas of social concern.

The leading effort at adjusting GNP has been made by Professors William Nordhaus and James Tobin of Yale who have tried to develop out of GNP something they call "MEW" or the "Measure of Economic Welfare." To convert GNP to MEW, they make a number of technical corrections, subtracting "regrettable" expenditures such as money spent for police protection and adding in currently unmeasured production, such as the value of leisure time activities.

The surprising thing is that the calculation, quite contrary to popular belief, shows that our Measure of Economic Welfare is not only higher than our national production but that the spread has been increasing. Figure III illustrates that, in effect, the studies of Nordhaus and Tobin seem to say that when you adjust Gross National Product for the quality of life, quality is improving even more rapidly than quantity.

The problems here are partly due to the fact that people fail to realize that GNP tries only to measure material goods that go through the market place. It does not measure, for

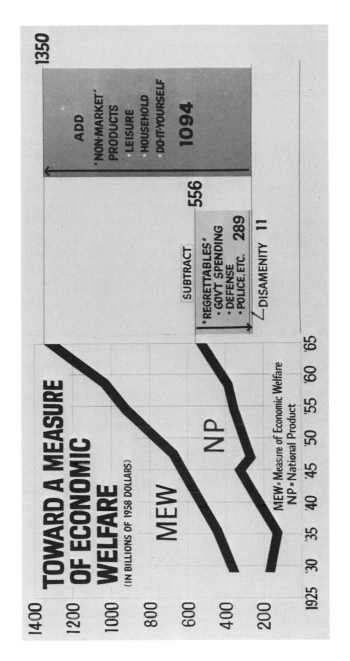

Figure III – *Toward a Measure of Economic Welfare*

example, household output. This means that if a bachelor marries his cook, national production goes down, because the allowance that a husband gives his wife does not pass through the market place while the payment to the cook does. On the contrary, if you divorce your wife and thereafter pay her to do your laundry, the Gross National Product goes up, because the allowance has now become a market payment for laundry. Similarly the decision to exclude illegal activities produces odd results. When the nation decided that the sale of alcoholic beverages was illegal, many saloons closed and others became speakeasies, but they all went out of the GNP until repeal of prohibition brought them back into the GNP.

The major deduction made by Nordhaus and Tobin is to exclude a category of so-called "Regrettable Expenditures" which do not contribute directly to the welfare of households. These include such items as national defense, police, etc. Why should the criminal's gun and crowbar, equally with the householder's burglar alarm system, be considered additions to national prosperity? Interestingly enough, after these additions and deductions and after a deduction for the deterioration of the environment (in an economist's terms, "after internalizing certain external social costs"), the MEW has been steadily rising during these current years of extraordinary public dissatisfaction. Even more refined calibration than this early attempt at MEW is necessary if the public debate is to be rational and informed and if the necessary trade-offs are to be recognized. In particular, the deduction to be made for deterioration of the environment is a controversial amount. But preliminary calibration—even if we quadruple the environmental deduction used by Nordhaus and Tobin—does suggest that the unconditional condemnation of economic growth by some academics, such as E. J. Mishan of the London School of Economics, is not supported by the data. As Simon Kuznets has recently said:

"The critics usually go overboard and undersell the value of growth. They don't realize that every generation has its external diseconomies—life in the 19th Century wasn't as good as they imagine."

Within a given total GNP, Peter must get less if Paul is to get more. This sort of transfer by taxation and welfare payment is simple economics, but it is politically complicated. Take one illustration of the complexity of such trade-offs. If to raise the total electric energy available in the nation, we must increase air pollution, a very baffling economic cost/benefit debate results. Air-conditioning improves the interior environment of the air-conditioned space but at two costs to the external environment. One cost is the impact of the heat and noise on the immediate neighbors of the air-conditioned building—whose only defense is to install air-conditioning themselves. The second cost is the necessary pollution at the point of electrical generation. It is easy enough to say that we are over-air-conditioned, particularly if those who say it spend their summers at Bar Harbor. But who is going to decide to hold down the total of electrical generation and who is going to ration the available electricity? The very same voters and politicians who as consumers keep buying and installing more and more air-conditioners! A recent Roper Report found that heavy majorities would pay 10% more for gasoline, automobiles and electricity if this was the only way to have purer air. "But some kinds of people are more willing than others to pay for purer air and water. Greatest enthusiasm is shown by the environmentally-sensitive young, and the affluent, who can best take the price in stride. Greatest resistance comes from people 50 and over and from people with low income."

Such polls which assume easy solutions for modest cost increases oversimplify the problem. Consider, for example, the necessary trade-offs between energy and pollution if we were to go along with some of the back-to-nature environmentalists. The maximum kilowatt demand in Pittsburgh last year was 2,015,000 KW. Translated into horsepower at .75 horsepower per kilowatt, this means that a return in Pittsburgh to horses instead of electric generation would require 2,700,000 horses in the area at peak need and 1,700,000 horses at average need. No one could believe that the quality of life in Pittsburgh would be improved by having 2,700,000 horses around, particularly when other sources of pollution such as automobiles remain the same. To further complicate the matter, the Department of Agriculture has pointed out that one-quarter of the crops harvested once went to feed animals used for power.

We simply do not have the farm land needed to support an animal-powered agriculture let alone an animal-powered industry. Our problem is to elevate the public understanding and the political debate to the point where trade-offs can be made and sensible balances be struck. We need more specific measures of "illfare" and welfare.

In the final days of the Lyndon Johnson presidency, the U.S. Department of Health, Education and Welfare published interim results of a three-year study looking toward the development of a Social Report for the United States. The study deals with such aspects of the quality of American life as: health and illness; social mobility; the physical environment; income and poverty; public order and safety; learning, science and art; and participation and alienation. In his transmittal letter of the report about three years ago, Secretary Wilbur J. Cohen of HEW stated that a first Social Report could be developed within two years. This has not been accomplished—in part because some experts, while concerned with making contemporary social science more useful for the function of social reporting, are not persuaded that the underlying measurements of social change have been sufficiently developed to justify the formality of an official Social Report.

Meanwhile, however, the Central Statistical Office of Great Britain has issued a publication called "Social Trends" intended to assemble official statistics to help public understanding and discussion of social policy on such subjects as welfare services, health, education, housing, justice and law, public expenditure, population and environment, employment, leisure, personal income and expenditures and social security. Such information can prevent us from finding ourselves in the position of the passengers on the airliner whose pilot reported that his compass was broken so they were lost, but that his clock was working and they were on schedule.

It is not easy to develop appropriate social indicators. No government, no educational institution, no church, has ever been able to come up with any measure of its performance half as simple and acceptable as GNP and corporate net profit have been for our society until just recently. How does the Catholic Pope measure his success or failure? Certainly the test is not whether the total money contributed rises or falls. Does he merely tabulate christenings? If so, he has little test of market penetration when vast populations of Mohammedans, Buddhists, Jews and atheists do not offer him a comparable measurement. Does he keep track of Catholic marriages? This is a rite of passage common to all faiths and civil governments. But it should be little satisfaction if the percentage of Catholic marriages to total marriages increases simply because an increasing number of the participants in the marriages are former priests and nuns. There are similar confusions in trying to calibrate the benefit of government expenditures. Most government programs thus far have measured merely dollars spent rather than results accomplished. For example, in the January 1969 "Economic Report of the President," Lyndon B. Johnson claimed "We have improved education for the young to enhance their productivity and their wisdom as citizens of a great democracy," but the evidence offered in the Report to support his claim was only in terms of expenditures and not in terms of a calibration of results. It is now common knowledge that within certain limits there is very little correlation between money spent and quality of education produced.

The argument over GNP versus other guides has led to the suggestion of Senator Mondale that we create a three-member Council of Social Advisors comparable to the Council of Economic Advisors created by the Employment Act of 1946. The new Council would be required to issue an annual social report to the nation and to a joint Congressional committee. In 1970 his bill passed the Senate, but not the House, and it has been reintroduced in the current Congress. Significantly, the Mondale bill was co-sponsored by 22 other Senators from both parties including among others, Senators Javits, Kennedy and Muskie.

In Senator Mondale's words, "The time has come for this nation to devote the same intense effort to analysis of its social trends and recommendations of techniques to deal with them, as it now devotes to economic description, analysis, prediction, and recommendation.

"The gulf between those who participate in the promise of America and those who cannot, cries out for a bridge, but we still do not know how long a bridge we need, or what it must be built of, or how to anchor it on either side of the abyss. Perhaps we will need more than one kind of bridge."

It is fortunate that the advances in social science and computer technology make us more capable of visualizing and quantifying our problems. But, as Senator Mondale urges, there must be a systematic and continuing process of acquiring and analyzing the relevant data. For example, Joseph A. Califano, principal domestic policy assistant in the Johnson White House has said: "The disturbing truth is that the basis of recommendations by an American cabinet officer on whether to begin, eliminate or expand vast social programs, more nearly resembles the intuitive judgement of a benevolent tribal chief in remote Africa than the elaborate sophisticated data with which the Secretary of Defense supports a major new weapons system. When one recognizes how many and how costly are the honest mistakes which have been made in the Defense Department, despite its sophisticated information systems, it becomes frightening to think of the mistakes which might be made on the domestic side of our Government because of lack of adequate data." And Califano also has related the experience he had when, in 1965, the Department of Health, Education, and Welfare wanted to know the composition of welfare rolls. There was—and still is—the myth that there are vast numbers of able-bodied men receiving welfare. Califano found that there simply was no immediate source of factual information. When the welfare data were finally obtained, it was learned that of the 7.3 million then on welfare, only 50,000—less than one-tenth of one per cent—were males who could possibly be called "able-bodied." The facts as opposed to the myth remain to be fully understood by the general public, but at least the officials most concerned with policy and administration are brought nearer to reality by the availability of such social statistics.

The Council of Economic Advisors has brought prestigious and sophisticated economic experts out of academia and into day-by-day economic policy disputes comparable to the debate on able-bodied welfare cases—thereby bringing to the public attention a body of informed viewpoints which elevates the level of public debate on questions of economic policy. Perhaps the Mondale Council of Social Advisors will similarly provide the quantification of concern, the social accounting, which will make possible a more scientific approach to social welfare—a better hope that we will reach those national goals beyond greater GNP.

All the above will, of course, affect the corporate manager in his role as citizen and taxpayer. The considerable interest, concern and attention to social accounting and social indicators in connection with national macrosociological procedures cannot fail to result in a similar interest becoming important in microeconomic analysis of large corporations. In addition, the compilation of national data will certainly require underlying corporate data. Thus, as we perfect on a national level a better measure than Gross National Product as an indication of national well-being, it will be necessary for individual corporations to develop better measures than "net profit per share after taxes" as an adequate measure of the firm's function as an institution of social and economic progress. But all that is the subject of tomorrow's lecture—"Social Responsibility—Some Corporate Purposes Beyond Maximum Net Profit."

II. Social Responsibility
Some Corporate Purposes
Beyond Maximum Net Profit

II. Social Responsibility
Some Corporate Purposes Beyond Maximum Net Profit

As we were coming into Skibo Hall this afternoon, I saw a sign advertising a poetry series at Carnegie-Mellon with Yevgeny Yevtushenko and Archibald MacLeish. It might be appropriate to start our discussion with a bit of verse so that those who wandered in here in the mistaken belief they were coming to a poetry reading will not be entirely disappointed. Back in my college days when I was trying out for the student newspaper, I carefully observed the best journalistic tradition: "If you can't find news, create it." In pursuit of this I persuaded a classmate to eat a relatively small live gold fish. The Boston *Transcript*, after the fun and excitement died down, ran a verse that went something like this:

> "To end this paranoiac prank, oh Harvard how we wish,
> You'd put the students in a tank and graduate the fish."

The tradition of such light verse in Boston is a long and honorable one. Our Boston Gas Company, which serves 31 cities and towns in the Boston area, was involved not so long ago in sponsoring a verse contest for children. The competition was intended to find creative young people who could put together extemporaneous verse. I was one of the judges. In the finals there were 31 youngsters, each from a different one of the communities we serve, who were asked under time pressure to create a bit of a verse that would emphasize the advantages of Boston Gas utility service and also mention their home town. The first youngster got up and read his little verse:

> "There was a girl from Concord, Mass.,
> Who cooked good food with Boston Gas.
> She had a gorgeous shape, a lot of class,
> And she waded out in Boston Harbor up to her knees."

I said to the young fellow, "I like the approach, but the last line doesn't rhyme." His reply was: "Mr. Goldston, you just wait until the tide comes in."

That really summarizes the underlying theme of my comments tonight. There is a changing tide in public attitudes, and business firms cannot afford to wait till the tide is fully in. In the first lecture we discussed the shift of public concern away from what we loosely call the "quantity" and toward the "quality" of life. We noted that GNP (Gross National Product) had lost favor as a measure of our national illfare or welfare. In this second lecture we move down a notch from the problems of the nation to the problems of a business firm and its traditional use of the figure we call net profit as its measure of corporate welfare or illfare.

We talk very frequently in Chamber of Commerce and Manufacturers Association meetings about the free enterprise system. But when we try to figure out what we really mean by the free enterprise system we find the traditional social justification of it expressed in three propositions that individually are probably not debatable.

The first proposition is that the effort by each individual firm to maximize its own profits results for society in an overall allocation of our productive resources, our machinery and our manpower, such that the material wants of society will be met not only at minimum costs but with some regard to social priority. The theory is that the market mechanism transmits to many competing individual firms the demands of people for the material things they want. The firms that meet these demands successfully should prosper, grow and become more profitable. Thus through some sort of an invisible hand, the resources of our society are directed toward those business institutions which meet society's needs at minimum cost and with maximum sensitivity to public demand.

The second proposition we use as a justification of the free enterprise system is that the continuing re-allocation of resources among different firms to the most efficient firms means that we will have a continuing increase in our total output and maximum utilization of our resources. Thus, in ideal operation of this process we will maintain an equilibrium somewhere near full employment.

The third proposition is that, given a market system and competition among firms, the role of government is merely to see that the system does not get clogged up by monopoly or deception or other practices which should be illegal because they impair the process which almost automatically will see that the needs of the society are met and that they are met at a minimum cost with a growing output.

As we discussed earlier, John Maynard Keynes, in 1936, challenged and revolutionized this economic theory by pointing out that we had arrived at an equilibrium with a substantial unemployment. The free enterprise system had balanced out with 16 million unemployed Americans. Following up Keynes' changes of economic theory and Kuznets' studies of how to measure our national output, Americans changed their notion of what government ought to do. It was decided that government had a more active role—that through taxation and expenditure the government could, and had a duty to, moderate cycles of prosperity and depression. This new economic theory that developed as a supplement to the traditional theory of free enterprise took many Americans quite a while to accept, because it contradicted our orthodox belief about what government ought to do and what taxes ought to be used for. But Keynesian economics was eventually pretty generally accepted and served us well until the 1960's.

Then John Kenneth Galbraith challenged Keynesian economics by pointing out that it was failing to solve a good many of our current social problems. Amidst great private affluence, there were pockets of poverty and in the public sector, dirty streets, inadequate jails and generally poor government services. Galbraith suggested that the market mechanism had been undermined by corporate planning as a rational method of allocating our productive resources. He challenged the belief that a rise in total income would necessarily improve total national welfare, pointing out that this rising tide does not lift all of the ships equally.

Faced with this challenge, businessmen cannot continue to cling to the classical economics they learned in college. With public opinion and public problems out ahead of the way you think and the way you act, you can become a sort of economic fossil, like Sewell Avery at Montgomery Ward hoarding for the post-war crash that didn't come or the original Henry Ford living out the twilight of his $5 day. On the other hand, even Keynesian economics (which President Nixon has finally been persuaded to adopt) will not suffice if public expectations of what business should do go far beyond what most of us think is the traditional role of business. In a recent study by The Committee for Economic Development there is a chapter headed "The Changing Social Contract with Business" which states, "Overall, a clear majority of the public thinks corporations have not been sufficiently concerned about the problems facing our society. Two-thirds believe business now has a moral obligation to help other major institutions to achieve social progress, even at the expense of profitability." That is worth emphasizing—about two-thirds of the general public feel that social responsibility should to some extent prevail over net profitability. But continuing from the C.E.D.: "The fact is that the public wants business to contribute a good deal more, (more than cheaper goods, more than less pollution and more than better jobs) to achieving the goals of a good society. . . . Business enterprises, in effect, are being asked to contribute more to the quality of American life than just supplying quantities of goods and services."

I might illustrate this shift in concern and change in attitude by a rather interesting experience in our company. About 10 or 12 years ago we had as our shareholders a relatively small group of professional investors. We wanted, like all growing American corporations, to broaden our shareholders' list. That was when the New York Stock Exchange was trying to persuade everybody that they should own a piece of Wall Street. We hired a professional consultant on investor relations. He dressed, and looked and acted like one of those fellows in an undertaking firm who directs the crowd at a funeral. This seemed rather appropriate because he emphasized to us that prosperous widows are really the most desirable kind of shareholder. They buy slowly and they never sell, and they follow the advice of people who are not hot-shot, go-getting stockbrokers, but conservative fellows like accountants and lawyers. Then he advised us to begin by changing the design of our stock certificate. I said, "What's the matter with the stock certificate?" He pulled it out and there was a beautiful, full-bosomed, stark-naked, goddess of industry, holding a cornucopia. He said, "You can't sell a stable shareholder list of prosperous widows with that kind of a thing." So we changed our stock certificate and we were pretty successful in enlarging our shareholders' list.

Recently the consultant got hold of us again and said that he had some new ideas for us. This time he said that a good many investment firms are setting up what they call socially-conscious investment funds. The Dreyfus Fund has established the Third Century Fund and there also is First Spectrum Fund, Inc., both planning to invest in firms which protect the environment. Our consultant said that these Funds will run around to churches and colleges and tell them that it is possible to make money and do good for society at the same time by investing in firms that offer "social responsibility" along with profitability and growth. We were a little startled. Our former staid-looking consultant now was really with it. He looked like a slightly disheveled Abraham Lincoln in floral beach pajamas, and he was saying to us, "You've lost touch with society. You've got to change your stock certificate." I said, "Now what's wrong with the stock certificate?" He replied, "Look what you've got on the stock certificate, a whole lot of factories with great big belching smokestacks. They look like they're not only putting out the effluent, it looks like a lot of product is going up the chimney." We decided to change the stock certificate, but in these days of permissive pornography, I'm not too sure what we're going to go to next.

There is something symbolic about this story. We are only one of a great many corporations engaged not only in removing the pictures of productive pollution from our stock certificates and advertisements, but also in trying to remove the pollution from our production. These are the felt demands of shifting national values—not that we tear up the stock certificates and hope for some kind of non-polluted socialism. Faith has really not been lost in the traditional corporate concern with profit, and indeed, confidence has not been lost in the market mechanism itself.

This is emphasized by the same C.E.D. studies which indicated that, so far as corporate charitable gifts were concerned, there was some feeling that enough, or perhaps even more than enough, was being done. The public desire clearly is not that the business firm give more, but that it act differently. It is not a question of generosity, it is a question of behavior. This probably reflects a public appreciation, with all the excited rhetoric about social responsibility, that there is a differential impact upon the world between what a company does and what it gives. We might illustrate that by taking a look at Figure IV, which is a pro forma income statement of an average large manufacturing company. A company with $100 million dollars in sales is likely to make, before federal income taxes, about $5 million. It will pay federal income taxes of about $2½ million. There will thus be a net profit for the shareholders of about $2½ million. It well might, in today's world, have about 2500 employees earning an average of $10,000 a year each for about a $25 million payroll. Fringes add $5 million to labor costs. There are other expenses for raw materials and energy,

THE ECONOMICS OF SOCIAL VALUE

SALES		**$100,000,000**
EXPENSES:		
LABOR COSTS		
2,500 MEN @ $10,000	$25,000,000	
FRINGES & PENSIONS	5,000,000	
OTHER EXPENSES		
RAW MATERIALS, ENERGY, DEPRECIATION, INTEREST, INSURANCE, etc.	61,950,000	
LOCAL & STATE TAXES	3,000,000	
CHARITABLE GIFTS		
1% OF PRE-TAX PROFIT	50,000	
		95,000,000
PRE-TAX PROFIT		$5,000,000
FEDERAL INCOME TAX		2,500,000
NET PROFIT		$2,500,000

50 × $10,000 = $500,000 + FRINGES & BENEFITS
$500,000 ÷ $50,000 = 10X BY WAGES
$2,500,000 ÷ $50,000 = 50X BY TAXES

Figure IV – *The Economics of Social Value*

depreciation, interest and the rest—almost $62 million. Local and state taxes today are easily 3% of sales, and in many businesses more. The usual corporate charitable gifts come to about 1% of pre-tax profit. The federal income tax law allows up to a 5% deduction, but many studies show that the average large corporation makes charitable gifts of about 1% of its pre-tax income. Suppose now that this company never had any black employees, but due to government pressure or social consciousness or what you will, it decided to hire black employees up to 2% of its work force. This means 50 minority employees earning $10,000 each for $500,000 of payroll plus fringes and benefits. Compare the social impact of that to the $50,000 given to charity—10 times as much. Compare the taxes of $2½ million—50 times as much as given to charity. It is perfectly clear that in terms of relative impact, the solution really is not to increase a corporation's charitable giving, but to divert some portion of that $95 million of other expenditures that come in and go out of the corporation toward helping achieve some of our social goals.

I do not want to suggest that it is unimportant to try to increase the charitable giving by corporations. If you somehow persuaded corporate management to double its charitable giving from 1% just to 2%, it would be the equivalent of creating four additional Ford Foundations. Although we are talking about relatively small percentages in charitable gifts, we are talking about important total dollars. The longer run strategy, however, should be to try to see that somehow the market mechanism that directs the allocations of resources heads the general corporate effort toward our social problem areas.

This may also be a good point at which to emphasize again that it is a rising total wealth that makes us more conscious of differences between rich and poor but also makes us better able to do something about them. If our $100 million company is not growing and has to displace 50 white employees to make places for the 50 new black employees, it becomes a zero sum game with just an income transfer—and an infinitely more difficult game for the manager to play—especially if he has a strong union. How much easier to hire 25% black in the next

200 employees being added. Similarly, how much easier to tax and transfer from an increase in GNP than from a stable GNP. Just imagine how much greater the tensions of the 1960's would have been if the gains of the blacks and the other disadvantaged had all had to come from a static total GNP.

It also seems to be becoming clearer except to the wildest of ecologists that the pollution problems come from a congested population and from cost considerations that affect non-profit and public institutions as much as they do profit-seeking corporations. Although it is the private corporation part of the pollution problem to which today's lecture is addressed, we must recognize that this is only part of the problem. The air pollution coming from the smokestacks of hospitals and schools and the water pollution from inadequate municipal sewage works is too apparent for the majority of Americans to link pollution exclusively to private ownership and net profit. They increasingly understand that in a congested society it becomes necessary to restrict the use of the public air and water as a cheap disposal system for both private and public enterprises. What I am suggesting is that we are only just beginning to make the public political decisions to internalize the costs of reducing pollution through an increase in taxes for this purpose, just as our market system has failed to force private firms to internalize these costs with the long-run consequence of higher prices. Lower net profits can only be a short-run consequence in a free enterprise economy.

We must make public decisions to spend more public funds on the externalized costs of public activities and—most difficult—we must teach and discipline our unruly public. For example, some ecologists are learning how hard it is to persuade the general public not to litter and are becoming pessimistic on legislation outlawing non-returnable bottles and mandating deposits as a solution to the litter problem. Consumers usually throw away returnable bottles along with the one-way types. The Pepsi Cola Company recently tried an experiment to assess public response to deposit charges. The company charged a 5 cent deposit on 14½ million 16-ounce bottles distributed in New York during the test period. Within less than a year, 11 million of the bottles disappeared from circulation, meaning that consumers forfeited more than $500,000 in deposits during that period. Actually, soft drink and beer companies feel compelled to offer one-way cans and bottles by what they judge to be public demand even though they find returnable bottles less expensive and more profitable.

Most companies, however, are not able to say that changes in public or their own behavior in response to ecological and other social demands will reduce their costs and add to their profit, thus producing no conflict between social responsibility and net profit. It is the usual fact of increased costs that creates a conflict between profit and social responsibility and raises for the professional manager of a public corporation the tough question: for whom is he managing the enterprise?

The theoretical niceties of this problem were debated 40 years ago in some classic articles by A. A. Berle and Merrick Dodd in the Harvard Law Review. Such niceties still trouble Milton Friedman who has argued in his well-known Sunday New York Times Magazine article that: "In a free-enterprise, private-property system a corporate executive is an employee of the owners of the business. He has direct responsibility to his employers. That responsibility is to conduct the business in accordance with their desires, which generally will be to make as much money as possible while conforming to the basic rules of the society, both those embodied in the law and those embodied in ethical custom."

The most popular theoretical reply to Professor Friedman has been proposed by Professors Wallick and McGowan in "A New Rationale for Corporate Social Policy" in which they argue that most stockholders hold equities either directly or indirectly in more than one company and so one can propose logically that the stockholder of Company A should be happy if A's lessened profit redounds to the general benefit of a nation, including the A stockholder's ownings in Companies B through Z. In a sense, the argument boils down to "what is good for the United States is good for General Motors' stockholders." But the heart of the debate is whether the corporate management has a constituency different from or beyond the traditional stockholder, who is assumed to want a maximum profit per share.

I believe one can reconcile Milton Friedman and the C.E.D. by reading into his phrase "while conforming to the rules of society" some of the "broadened expectations" found by the C.E.D. After all, Friedman doesn't feel that the manager's duty to the shareholder requires him to violate safety or tax legislation or to do things that, while profitable and not illegal, would shock community conscience—such as refusing to contribute anything at all to local charities or doing only the absolute minimum that obsolete laws require for employee health and safety. The C.E.D. has verified the trend and present state of what they call "public opinion" and what Friedman calls "rules of society." Now perhaps there is some gap or no man's land between these two concepts—or at least between how Friedman and the C.E.D. would each separately appraise them—but, if so, it is a gap easy enough for any manager to rationalize whichever way it suits him. The trouble with Professor Friedman's approach is that it assumes too much exactness as to rules of society and also as to net profit. Economists often have a delusion of certainty about net profit and "the bottom line" which parallels the delusion of many non-economists that GNP is a measure of great precision.

But any experienced corporate manager knows that net profit figures can be managed as often for reasons of accuracy as for reasons of deception. Most important, the exactness of any quantification is limited by the arbitrariness of the accounting period. For enterprises with long lived assets, deferred taxation and complicated and even convertible capital structures, net profit per share in terms of quarters or even years is a pretty delusive figure. Management has more discretion with it than most C.P.A.'s will readily admit. Most publicly held firms would regard themselves as imprudent if they did not have up the treasurer's sleeve items which could raise or lower net profit by the equivalent of at least a quarter and preferably 6 months' earnings. There are many instances where accounting judgements have altered earnings far in excess of that. The more complex the company, the more controllable the reported profit for an arbitrary time period.

The point I am making is that too naive a belief in the precision of net profit leads us into two errors. First, the error of assuming that the financial health of an enterprise can be sufficiently measured by the reported net profit. Second, the error of discarding efforts at corporate social accounting just because they lack precision.

Penn Central is not the only corporate fatality whose reported and audited book net profit failed to forewarn of disaster. As a matter of fact, the best indication I know of the failing or improving health of a marginal corporation is the decrease or increase of its United Way contribution—particularly because it is the modest-sized profit which is most easily nudged up or down by a large percentage. The neighboring supplier or customer or competitor who has the firm's United Way card is likely to know by local trade gossip how well his prospect is actually doing.

One is reminded of the story of the Carnegie-Mellon business graduate who returned to work in his father's clothing store and soon began to complain about the hopeless bookkeeping. "Dad, you can't tell whether you're making money on women's dresses and losing it on men's suits. You don't control or even record markdowns. How can you tell if you're making a profit?" To which the impatient father replied by grabbing 4 pairs of pants, 2 overcoats and 6 dresses, and screaming, "For that I sent you to Carnegie-Mellon! What I'm holding is what I started with. All the rest is net profit."

We must be careful, however, not to be led into a misunderstanding of the dynamics of contemporary publicly owned corporations just because we conclude that the net profit calculation is a little murky. Once you decide that long-term net profit cannot be calculated very accurately and that management today is expected to spend a lot of the company time and money on charities, training hard core blacks, and plant beautification, you can easily conclude that managers really don't care much about profits at all. This leads you on to Kenneth Galbraith's concept of the New Industrial State where the impregnable management technostructure tosses the shareholders enough crumbs to keep them quiescent and runs the company largely for its own purposes.

This is the reading or—to my mind—the misreading of some of the modern organization theory which treats the firm as a coalition (managers, workers, stockholders, suppliers, customers) whose members have conflicting demands that must be reconciled if the firm is to survive. The managers, according to some theories, then operate the firm largely in their own self-interest, keeping the other coalition members quiet by paying them what becomes necessary. With the shareholders, in particular, management does not try to maximize profits but merely "satisfices"—that is, it tries to make satisfactory profits the way a student in pass-fail grading might try merely not to fail rather than try to get the highest grade in the class.

There is a good deal of truth in the proposition that managements of large public corporations satisfice, but this, I think, avoids the real issue of management motivation. For most of the corporations most of the time, the necessity to earn more this year than last year is a pervasive rule of thumb though not an exclusive motive.

There is, however, an important distinction between satisficing at a high rate of earnings growth and maximizing each transaction: maximizing leaves no room for management to be less than a Scrooge exacting the last penny in each transaction. Satisficing at a growth rate suggests that a leadership position can be taken at some cost in net profit but only after hurdling each year a higher and higher test of satisfactory earnings. This distinction between satisficing at a growth rate and maximizing may seem to be just a matter of words, but it goes to the heart of how the profit seeking public corporation can be housebroken to behave differently in a society with changing values.

Corporations do not have motives except as their top management selects targets and goals. I have elsewhere argued in detail my personal observation that it is not total net profit but rather growing net profit per share which is currently the primary motivating force for managers of American public corporations. Although the management teams usually own only a small percentage of most public companies, this small percentage of the company is often pretty nearly 100% of their own property, and its value as affected by earnings is therefore of great personal importance. For example, a 1970 study showed that the chief executive officer of a large publicly-owned corporation typically owned stock in it with a market value of about $1,000,000. Many executive compensation plans are based on earnings. (President James Roche of General Motors took a personal $400,000 pay cut in 1970 when the General Motors bonus plan reflected the impact on earnings of the 1970 auto strike.) Stock options typically limited to five years put great pressure on management to improve earnings in the short run. With five security analysts for every listed company, even quarterly earnings reports are analyzed and debated with resultant stock market sensitivity. In addition, there are social pressures on the executive of a public corporation. His friends, housekeeper and barber will invest in his company because "everyone ought to be a little way into Wall Street" and it is the only company whose name they know. Soon every cocktail party will be a shareholders' meeting and a shareholder-barber with a razor at your throat will be asking about the decline in the last quarter's earnings.

Professional managers also know that, hard as net profit may be to define, it is the way our economy has come to allocate the capital needed for growth. The retained earnings, the money that banks will lend or bond underwriters will raise, the stock you can sell at good prices or use in acquisitions—all these sources of capital start to close down when earnings decline or even fail to grow. As a result, whenever a particular product or a particular industry becomes profitable, there is a movement of more resources (including human resources) into that product or industry and away from products and industries with declining or stable profits. This has proved to be an extraordinarily efficient mechanism for decentralized resource allocation. The extreme alternative is allocation by a vast bureaucracy. In the effort to meet social problems to which this mechanism is currently failing to allocate adequate resources, it is important that we recognize how fundamental the pressure for net profit is to the proper working of our mechanism for resource allocation. Otherwise we may foul up our delicate system which continuously reorganizes industry for improved productivity and rising output. What we must seek are techniques of guiding the economy by way of net profit and the market—including accounting, disclosure, taxes, penalties and incentives—which will bring about the kind of public and corporate behavior that we want but still allow decentralized decisions as to resource allocation.

In view of the competitive atmosphere within which most American business executives grew up, one can scarcely overestimate the importance of requiring a scoreboard for performance. For most professional executives, the profit figure not only satisfies personal avarice but also satisfies a desire to quantify the team performance and to measure it against the performance of other teams. I am suggesting that when we put other items in addition to net profit upon that scoreboard, the team will respond by adding to its objectives. We have already seen how well changing some of the rules and some of the scorekeeping works out in our national sports. When football injuries resulted in public concern, the rules were changed so as to reduce injuries. The scorekeeping was also altered. The result is not to reduce the effort put in by the players, but rather to modify tactics and change objectives. If, for example, field goals are given a higher score and clipping is given a higher penalty, there will be more efforts for field goals and fewer clipping attempts.

We must not overdo the degree to which motives of increasing profit rather than satisficing motives determine many management actions. After all, there are at least ten groups top management must consider in addition to stockholders: (1) lenders, (2) non-management employees, (3) managers, (4) retired management and non-management employees, (5) customers, (6) suppliers, (7) competitors, (8) government, (9) neighbors or local communities and (10) society in general.

In our own corporate experience, each category tends to regard itself as primary and the individual thinks of his personal needs before he considers those of his group. For example, a social responsibility test-run of interviews and questionnaires used on a large segment of management and non-management employees at one firm produced questions and answers like this:

Question:	Should we do business in countries such as South Africa or Greece?
Comment:	My room air-conditioner doesn't work and the window is stuck. I'd probably be more comfortable in South Africa.
Question:	Should we hire more disadvantaged people even at the expense of lower profits?
Comment:	Before we do anything else we should pave the parking lot. It's a mess now and will be worse by winter.

I suppose we should have expected that each of us wants relief for the blister caused by our own new shoes before we worry about the barefoot native in some far-off land, but the degree to which top management alone seems worried about social responsibility does suggest that the corporate changes ahead may not be glacial but they will be slow.

Another situation we found was the confusion of those who fit in several categories. For example, during the railroad strike last summer we kept one of our coal mines operating after storage bins had been filled, by piling the output on space we owned next to the cleaning plant in the middle of a little mining town, after having talked the problem over with the town officials and doing what we could to hold the dust down. I was visiting the area and while viewing the pile was told by a couple of ladies that it was simply awful to pile the coal up in the middle of the town. Suspecting that their husbands worked in the mine, I explained that the choice was to lay off the work force or pile up the coal, to which one lady immediately replied, "Look, mister, you keep the men working and when you run out of space there just come over and pile it up in my kitchen." Corporate managers are not the only ones who face conflict of interest problems—even the neighbor who is also an employee finds himself wearing two hats.

Just as with the choice between a single MEW or numerous social indicators for the nation, we can try to develop either some sort of an aggregate good citizen grade or a series of unrelated measures of social performance for the corporation. Both are being tried. A group of Stanford students is grading the canning industry on various activities, weighting the activities and deriving some sort of pass or fail grade for the firms. Is bigotry in employment five times or 50 times as bad or is it better than water pollution? The problems are endless and largely subjective. Most of us who have examined the alternatives have decided in favor of indicators, rather than some single aggregated figure, partly because most firms, like most people, are fairly consistently good or fairly consistently bad. People who wear clean shirts usually wear clean underwear—and vice versa. Thus a few indicators often can be as significant as a massive investigation with careful weighting of apples and oranges.

The recent "black lung" experience in the coal industry is an illustration of why calibration of problems is most essential and how even honest and dedicated people can both be misled by and learn from figures. When concern about dust levels in the coal mines began to become a political and a public issue, being an important coal mining firm, we of course looked into it and learned—or thought we learned—three things: (1) many but not all of the leaders were politically motivated and a few were a little nutty, (2) dust could not be measured and (3) there was no evidence it harmed health. Indeed, the only valid correlations of "black lung" (or pneumoconiosis) were with heavy cigarette smoking. What was called for, I suppose in retrospect, was a social audit, but our management people who worked inside the mines themselves were as certain of the facts as the absentee executives, and so I went back to Boston convinced that nutty or ambitious outside agitators had again raised an imaginary issue. There I came across a liberal magazine with an article by a Harvard psychiatrist who had spent a few days in Appalachia, denouncing the coal operators on the "black lung" issue. He was 75% wrong on anything that I knew about but this suggested that he might be 25% right on "black lung" and, if so, we did have a problem. This led us to a public health specialist who explained the heavy smoker correlation. In most industries where masks or respirators must be used, smoking is restricted or forbidden because the dust or fumes may ignite. Heavy smokers tend to chew tobacco or take snuff while in a place where they are not allowed to smoke, and so they tend to make least use of the masks or respirators since these interfere with the chewing. Thus the correlation of heavy smoking and "black lung" emphasized the dangerous fact that those most susceptible took the least precautions.

Meanwhile we learned that the British had been using measuring devices and had developed some ways to control the dust. We then publicly announced that whether or not the proposed law was passed, we were going to bring down the dust levels in our mines. When the measuring devices arrived and were put to use, we and most of the industry were embarrassed. Many of our working faces were already below the dust levels we had sworn could not be reached. Today, admittedly after considerable expense and effort, we are generally able to comply with a test considerably stricter than the one we volunteered to observe two years ago. Oddly enough, one cause of dust is dull cutting bits which rub rather than rip the coal. Sharp bits obviously also raise productivity while lowering dust, so in this instance both greater safety and higher productivity resulted from a single change in operations.

We keep coming back, then, to problems of quantification. Andrew Brimmer, a Governor of the Federal Reserve System, has pointed out how fundamentally important it is for business to start keeping track of and disclosing some of the company costs which ultimately raise prices and become social costs. Everyone seems to want cleaner air and more electric power. Until the price tag is put on this and taken to the regulatory authorities, however, no realistic trade-offs are possible. These are complicated and easily misunderstood matters.

Much of the resistance to recording and disclosing will be about the same as the early arguments under the SEC—and it is still said on financial reporting that SEC regulations, like hot pants, require the disclosure of much that is interesting but permit the non-disclosure of all that is vital. But even accounting and disclosure are not enough. Some sort of independent audit is necessary to review the very loose sort of social accounting which is already being done by individual corporations. For example, in the last two or three years the annual reports of numerous companies have emphasized (with text and pictures) the employment of blacks, the reduction of pollution, and other aspects of "social responsibility." It is to be suspected that a careful audit of the increase in pictures and text as opposed to an audit of the actual things being done would prove that the rhetorical and pictorial annual reports are misleading to an extent that would not be regarded as permissible in financial accounts. This is somewhat comparable to the motorcycle-riding, black carpenters that a multi-site builder in New York City was accused of having moved to each job ahead of a slower moving Federal inspection team.

Turning back to our Sultan, if he is to be a statesman as well as a Sybarite, he will be expected to be able to report on more than the degree to which his harem satisfied his appetites for beauty and for fine food. How many of that 35-member platoon of ladies are helping out as school volunteers? How many of them are littering the neighborhood with waste? How many of them are participating personally and as instructors in birth control programs? These are the new questions, the new accountings and the new challenges that the harem ledgers of the Sultan or a modern industrial state must be able to answer.

But how does society organize the interface of government with the market and the net profit mechanism of resource allocation so as better to achieve the shifting goals of life quality rather than life quantity? Can chances for profit in helping to solve social problems be increased, thereby increasing the chances of solving the problems? My final lecture will not give the answers but it will explore these questions.

III. Social Audit
Some National Goals and Corporate Purposes
Beyond Calibration

III. Social Audit

*Some National Goals and Corporate Purposes
Beyond Calibration*

The general thesis of these lectures is that our social expectations are changing in many ways and, as a consequence, the institutions of society have to change—not disappear, but change—and the ways we measure things have to change. Coming from Boston, the home of the bean and the cod, I am reminded of a story about the impact of the changing tides of ethnic population in New England. There used to be a popular verse in Boston:

"This is the city of Boston,
The home of the bean and the cod,
Where the Lowells speak only to the Cabots,
And the Cabots speak only to God."

The old Yankee families who had settled the territory, never really recognizing that the Indians had been there first, regarded themselves as the original settlers and did not welcome the arrival of the Irish and the Italians and the Jews and others who began to move into New England. A myth developed, on the other hand, amongst the newer groups that if you wanted to be a senator, or governor or president of a bank, or own a big department store, it was very helpful if your name was Saltonstall or Alden or Standish or Lowell or Cabot. It seemed very simple to solve the problem of upward mobility by just changing your name. So lots of people decided to change their names. In Massachusetts, the judicial procedure required that you go to court to get your name changed, and the case always came up before Judge Saltonstall or Judge Lowell. The Old Settlers' Society regularly opposed name changes on the grounds of public health or public welfare—the kinds of opposition that any form of social change always provokes—and for many years The Old Settlers' Society won all its cases. Then came the unhappy moment when an Irishman was elected Governor. In Massachusetts the definition of a judge is a lawyer who knew a governor, so Italian Joe Antonelli was appointed a judge by his old friend the Irish governor.

This led some of the newer citizens to try name changing cases again. A gentleman named Cohen decided he wanted to be a Cabot. And a fellow named Levinson decided he would like to be a Lowell. The Old Settlers' Society opposed again, but this time the case came before Judge Antonelli. He found in favor of the name change, and the Boston newspapers ran a revised edition of the verse:

"This is the city of Boston,
The home of the bean and the cod,
Where the Cabots speak only to the Lowells,
But they converse in Yiddish, by God."

This change in Boston typifies the underlying thesis of these lectures. The impact on all of us of structural changes in society will be the realization that you will no longer always win what you used to win. The rules of the game and the judges of the game and the scorekeeping of the game are beginning to change.

The two earlier lectures discussed how social problems to which inadequate resources are being allocated by our political and economic systems have become the focus of public interest and debate. The arguments at either extreme get us nowhere. Some of my industrialist friends seem to think that the ecology movement is made up entirely of hippies with limburger cheese on their mustaches who run around sniffing the air and finding that the whole country stinks. On the other hand, some of my professional and academic friends seem to think that business managers could if they wished restore the American environment to conditions that those Yankees on the Mayflower found, even though we have become an industrialized, urbanized and heavily populated nation. Between these extremes, millions—tens of millions—of thoughtful and practical people, however, recognize that we must begin a whole series of cost-benefit calculations and trade-offs, agree upon national goals and priorities, and then try to implement the decisions within the machinery of our political and economic systems.

This must be done at a time when a revolution in the Thomas S. Kuhn sense is occurring in economic theory and when public attitudes toward the proper social function of the corporation are changing. A substantial majority of the people have decided that government economic policy, working in large part through publicly owned corporations, can solve or at least ameliorate many social problems. Many economists and social scientists agree that our accumulated wealth and wisdom make this possible. And the proof seems to be at hand in the vastly better level of material life which resulted for America when the ideas of Keynes and the statistics of Kuznets were applied to level out prosperity and depression. Corporate management cannot afford to assume that better plant security and a larger public relations budget will permit all other activities to continue as before. A time comes when The Old Settlers' Society can't win. As Keynes himself said toward the end of his General Theory: "Practical men, who believe themselves to be quite exempt from any intellectual influences, are usually the slaves of some defunct economist. Madmen in authority who hear voices in the air are distilling their frenzy from some academic scribbler of a few years back. I am sure that the power of vested interests is vastly exaggerated compared with the gradual encroachment of ideas."

The heart of the matter, as I have tried to point out in the two earlier lectures, is that the classical justification of the free enterprise system has been that it provides a decentralized allocation of resources which produces efficiency and growth in material goods fairly responsive to public desires. The machinery for this is the operation within a free market of many firms, each seeking maximum profit for its owners. The classical role of government has been to see that the machinery is not clogged by monopoly or unfair trade practices. In the 1930's the American public changed its idea about the role of *government*, bringing dramatic changes to the interface of government and business. In the 1960's the American public began to change its idea of the role of the *corporation*, and we are beginning to struggle with the resulting problems of "social responsibility."

The call for social responsibility in this context becomes more than a faddish cliche. It represents a durable trend in public opinion which will require the business manager to shift some of his attention from his own firm's efficiency and competitive viability to the functioning and social viability of the publicly owned corporation in a democratic capitalist society. Some critics of business are already calling for the "Nuremberg Rule" of personal responsibility to be applied to every manager whose firm behaves in a fashion which displeases the critic. There are some areas of managerial personal wrongdoing such as the electric equipment price-fixing cases, but it is the working of our whole political and economic system rather than individual choices which must be considered when we change our social values. The individual firm, pressed by both domestic and foreign competition, has limited ability to incur dramatic increases in cost not simultaneously incurred by its competitors.

It is very important that the public debate on social responsibility recognize these political and economic realities. Otherwise we will blame the wrong part of the machinery for causing the problem and solve nothing by trying to replace or repair something that is not at fault.

Medical care begins with diagnosis, and diagnosis begins with measurement—temperature, pulse, heartbeat and the rest. But too many doctors of social ills seem to think that measurement is all that is required, except, perhaps, for a dose of denunciation. They would measure the pollution, the poverty, the discrimination; blame the problems on the establishment or the system; and then feel their task is done. But no disease was ever cured just by the application of a stethoscope or the insertion of a thermometer. The three tough steps must follow—diagnosis, prescription and administration of the cure. The further problem in a democratic society is that the citizen must be both patient and doctor—we must not only prescribe but we must also swallow our own medicine.

With this we have reviewed the two earlier lectures and stated the conflict between profit and what is loosely called "social responsibility." Now permit me to advance and then discuss five propositions which, it seems to me, will help in the search for remedies:

(1) The selection of goals and priorities is a public political decision. The business manager participates as just another voting citizen and argues his special interests as just another affected party.

(2) Government budgets, particularly the Federal budget, are the principal expression of our goals and priorities.

(3) The private firm responds to the carrot of profit and the whip of cost, but exhortation of managers can be effective within a limited range.

(4) As our values change, we need new measures of national and of corporate performance.

(5) The performance reports must be reviewed by outside auditors, but some matters are beyond quantification and can be checked only by field inspection.

Let us turn then to the selection of national goals and priorities. America has always been an undisciplined and an unplanned society. In recent years, we have let things get particularly bad in air and water pollution and in our central cities. And America has been an unprepared society. Until our problems become acute, we usually do not begin the first steps of formulating national goals or even national policies. But on a national level the broad outlines of our social problems are becoming apparent and the measurement of them is improving. We still lack mass media coverage and general awareness of the dimensions of these problems and of how great the costs of solution will be.

In many cases there is little understanding of how the problem arose—which means there is little understanding of how to solve the problem. We do not so much lack agreement on goals as we lack agreement on facts. We are just beginning to accumulate and publicize the social facts needed for establishing goals. As I said in the first lecture, the British now publish a far more comprehensive set of national social statistics than we do, and Denmark is almost as advanced as Britain in its plans for collecting social statistics. If we lack the facts and sound analysis of them, we will label the wrong actors as the evil devils, and exorcizing the wrong devils will not remedy much. Take, for example, the assertion often made that private enterprise was the principal villain in creating what has become known as the urban crisis. Scholars are just now sorting out the evidence and they are concluding that government policy rather than business was the primary offender in creating the urban crisis.

Until World War II our cities grew with some logical relationship between population, economics and structure of government. The steel industry grew in Pittsburgh and both immigrants from Europe and country people from Ohio and Pennsylvania came to Pittsburgh for jobs in the city and homes in the city. The garment industry and other light manufacturing grew in New York and New Jersey, and from both foreign lands and the American countryside people came to New York and to Newark to find jobs within the city and to build homes within the city. All sorts of people came to our cities—Gentile and Jew, native born and foreign. Only Orientals and Negroes were largely excluded from coming to America by our immigration laws. And not only our nation but also our cities believed the poem by Emma Lazarus that we inscribed on the pedestal of the Statue of Liberty:

"Give me your tired, your poor,
Your huddled masses yearning to breathe free,
The wretched refuse of your teeming shore,
Send these, the homeless, tempest-tossed to me;
I lift my lamp beside the golden door."

That wasn't a very selective migration—"tired, poor, wretched, homeless, tempest-tossed." And, of course, these migrants found in our cities poverty, discrimination, exploitation, and all the rest. The melting pot did not work too well, there were periods of social turmoil, municipal corruption flourished; but no one until after World War II spoke of city government as beyond management and no one spoke of central cities as beyond hope.

What happened after World War II to the growth of our cities? As was true of the earlier urbanization, people came to the city because they thought it would offer a better life than their old home. What was different after World War II? We are just beginning to accumulate the social statistics, and the analysis of them seems to show that we have had four distinct immense streams of migration since World War II, three of which have been handled quite successfully.

The first stream came from abroad and was limited and selective. In two instances, the Hungarian refugees of the 1950's and the Cubans of the 1960's, the Federal government set up rather successful resettlement programs. Our present urban crisis clearly is *not* caused by an inability to absorb foreigners—unless you list Puerto Ricans as foreigners and we will come to that later.

The second migration stream was white and it came from the American countryside. Almost three-quarters of the domestic rural-to-urban migration was caused by the fact that our rural birth rate has been running about double the urban birth rate. Even if rural employment had remained stable, a vast flow of people would have had to leave the countryside to find employment. Since rural employment in fact declined, there was a torrent of white migrants to the cities and the growing suburbs. But we usually forget that the cities and suburbs absorbed this torrent quite successfully.

The third successful migration stream was from the city proper to the suburbs. Oh, we complain about the crack in the picture window and how the problems of the city are penetrating suburbia. But no one would suggest that the new cities on Long Island have basic problems at all equal to those of New York City. On the other hand, as this white middle class exodus grew, it took from the city proper much of its tax base, its stable voters, its vitality. And as business moved from the central city to the new suburbs, the job opportunities in private firms became scattered away from the older city.

The fourth and thus far unsuccessful migration stream has been the minority groups—mainly rural blacks, but in some areas Puerto Ricans, Mexican Americans and American Indians. Even though this fourth migrant flow is less than 20% of the total, it was directed by discriminatory housing practices almost entirely into the central city areas at a time when jobs in private industry were moving to the suburbs. Although the previous urban poor had been different and unskilled, now they also were color-coded. The unskilled jobs were vanishing to the suburbs, and mass transportation didn't connect the ghetto and the jobs.

We experienced something quite unlike that earlier city growth when both new jobs and new homes were found in the city proper. At that time the municipal tax base expanded with new factories, new stores and new apartment houses. After World War II the cities increasingly were filling up with the disadvantaged and the discriminated against. Municipal growth had, indeed, become cancerous rather than benign. Thus the urban crisis came upon us.

Unfortunately, as a society, we had no apparatus to measure and to analyze this crisis as it developed. Therefore we had no national policy against which individual programs, whether of government or of business, could be tested. Of course, we can look at it the other way—because we had no policy we therefore had no statistics. We measure what we care about. And we do something about things whose dimensions are understood. As a matter of fact, as we now are beginning to realize, most of our government programs made the growing crisis worse. We gave FHA mortgages mostly in the suburbs. We built highways to facilitate commuting from the suburbs. We permitted welfare differences that encouraged the poor to migrate from the countryside to the cities. Business as well as the other sectors of our society participated as citizens in ignoring the growing problem and tolerating the unsound programs which pushed our central cities into crisis. And business moved plants from the central city to the suburbs which meant that white residents moved out to follow their jobs, and white, but not black, migrants from the countryside could find homes with easy transportation to work. But it is an exaggeration to say that business was the primary villain. No one in government or in the universities was predicting the coming crisis, and government programs such as urban renewal encouraged what business did by offering incentives to move and by condemning old central city plants. Our cities may indeed be a pretty awful mess today but the free enterprise system in itself did not make them what they are; it took a whole series of small and medium size decisions by government agencies and business firms which did not add up to a big overall wise social decision. Most of the incentives fed into the market by the government induced just the wrong sort of private firm response.

Indeed, the point of this discussion of the urban crisis in the context of national goals is to emphasize the fallacy of believing that the sum total of many individual decisions is the equivalent of a social decision. You may decide that competition between individuals will maximize effort, but you must also decide the framework within which the competition is to occur. You may also decide to use government programs to stimulate private activity, but you must also look at how the system will transmit the incentives and consider the secondary effects as well as the immediate problem.

But, as I said earlier, in a democracy the citizens are both doctor and patient. They must prescribe their own medicine—and for the national and local problems we have been discussing the medicine is restriction of free choice and increased taxation. This may mean a compulsory integration of suburbs and it may mean a lower standard of living in terms of personal material goods (by way of taxation) to provide a higher quality of life in the public area.

It is by no means clear that there is a public readiness to pay the cost of these trade-offs which are needed for the solution of the social problems with which we are currently concerned. It is by no means clear that there is a popular desire to preserve the central city by those who are not part of the elite and therefore do not have clubs, offices and cultural institutions there. It is by no means clear that the middle class desire for honest government without cronies and nepotism is shared by lower class citizens. Certainly the movement to curtail economic growth is largely made up of people who have all they want rather than those who await their first auto or T.V. set. Despite the limits of the market in allocating resources to public sector needs, because of the recent defeats of school and public facility bond issues, one wonders if without great national leadership we will make the political decision to withdraw resources from private consumption for public services. Many people when it comes to taxes as a cure seem to prefer the disease. They are like the man who was told by his doctor that he would lose his hearing if he continued to use alcohol. A few weeks later the doctor ran into his patient at a cocktail party ordering a double scotch on the rocks. When chided by his doctor, the patient replied: "I've thought it over very carefully and decided that I like what I drink much more than I like what I hear."

There are various theories as to why we have a similar attitude of disliking taxes more than we dislike the community problems which tax money can solve. Some economists blame the pervasive advertising which vigorously sells automobiles, toothpastes and deodorants but doesn't push higher taxes and the civic amenities these will buy. Others blame the structure where *my* higher taxes will purchase only a diffuse benefit such as better jails rather than my specific benefit of an air-conditioner. It has been said that truth is never black or white but often a variegated rainbow and often just grey. Probably both theories have some truth but the larger political problem, I think, is illustrated by Figure V, which shows that about 40 years ago a high majority of the voters were not taxpayers. In more recent years, almost all the voters are substantial taxpayers. Indeed, there are more people who pay taxes than people who vote. When the highest income group is already taxed at fairly high rates, the cry cannot be "soak the rich and give it to the poor." It becomes "why should we working people support the welfare people?" The job of economic and social understanding and of political persuasion then becomes so difficult that governments resort to lotteries and the sorts of obscure revenue sources that conceal the real issues of goals and priorities.

After all, government budgets are the calibration of how we have chosen to reconcile the interests and goals and values of different groups and classes in our society. The clearest statement of the reconciliation or lack of it is done in dollars in our National Budget. We can measure the priorities we have given different issues by the increases and decreases and even omissions in the National Budget.

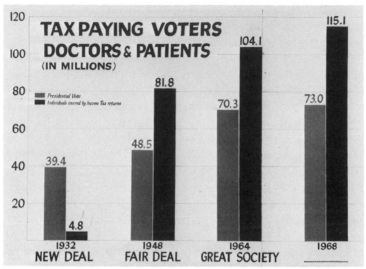

Figure V – *Taxpaying Voters–Doctors & Patients*

The Urban Coalition has issued a Counter Budget to highlight the options we have not taken. Emphasizing the importance of starting out with measurement, the Urban Coalition says:

"Persuading others to accept our priorities is not our primary purpose. Instead, we wish to stimulate a vastly more informed public debate on what national priorities ought to be. If we succeed in raising 'reordering national priorities' from its present status as a near-cliche to a topic marked by meaningful and disciplined discussion, we will consider our efforts a success."

Recent improvements in format of the National Budget and in secondary materials such as the Counter Budget which make the policy issues clearer have not, however, been accompanied by essential reforms in the way Congress considers the budget. Neither the categories into which the budget is divided for Congressional action nor the Congressional process of considering particular public programs and projects without weighing alternative public or private allocation of the resources can produce coherent Congressional debate or intelligent public discussion. Professor

Francis M. Bator has called for reform of procedure, machinery and ground rules, saying:

"Taxes and spending are instruments, not good or bad in themselves. When we decide about them, we are in effect deciding not only the balance between total demand and capacity, but also about how much of our resources to devote to such public tasks as defense, education, cities, and to helping the poor and the old and the sick, and how much to leave over for private investment and the personal consumption of people able to help themselves.

"These choices are among the most important that we as a community must make year by year. People will disagree about what the balance should be. We have no alternative but to compromise these differences through our politics. But one thing is plain. If we are to make these choices wisely, we must not be governed by arbitrary rules about what the government can afford at existing tax rates, or by cliches about the evils of taxes and public spending and government inefficiency. Rather, we must debate the choices for what they are, the dividing up of scarce means among various important public uses on the one hand and private uses on the other.

"...But it is not a matter of what we can afford. Rather it is a matter of what we as a very rich community—with a minority that is still very poor—want and need for a decent and a humane life."

The enormous progress that has been made in restructuring the budget by purpose is frustrated when it is introduced and debated in pieces rather than as an articulation of overall goals and priorities.

As revenue sharing becomes a more popular concept, it will become important to reform the state and local budget format and legislative procedures. In only a few states and cities does the citizen or even the legislator or the councilman have a budget format which can be said to articulate the social decisions which it contains. Again we must remember that people measure things they care about and begin to do something about things whose dimensions they can understand. As our state and local budgets become coherent, we will increasingly realize that in our urbanizing nation it is local government which is least able to cope with its problems. It will become even clearer that our fragmented and obsolete forms of municipal and state government cannot contend with forces reaching far beyond city and state borders. The maximum feasible participation of the poor will stir up the disadvantaged and make elected officials more aware of needs. But without resources and without a system to deliver them, this results not in solution but in indignation.

Unless we are prepared to await a change in human nature or the arrival of a political leader who can persuade the middle class to transfer part of its share of the GNP to the less advantaged, our best solution would seem to be to increase productivity and the grand total to be distributed, so that the resulting increment in annual wealth can be distributed more to the poor while merely slowing down the rate of growth in prosperity of the middle income voters. Even fairer sharing of the increment may be difficult to accomplish without education early in life about the relationship of economic and social issues.

It is important to have substantial funds allocated to these problem areas because the market mechanism will then through the profit motive attract private firms into attempting to solve many of the problems. The initiative must be a political decision on goals and priorities expressed by budget allocations. The response by private corporations will be immediate since many have already prepared themselves. As we have seen in the CED studies, public opinion is expecting just this attention to our social programs by large corporations. But, as my firm and many others have learned in the past few years, until society's needs and desires are in fact reflected by an effective demand—the ability to order and pay for—there is little the private firm can do.

Take, for example, my own company's efforts in solid waste disposal. Through our gas distribution company we know a good deal about cities and how they work. Through our barge line we know a great deal about transporting bulky, low-value material. Through our coal mining company we know a great deal about earth moving. And so we developed the concept of "Earthguard I." We would compact solid wastes—trash and garbage—in a huge press to about the same density as coal. The resultant slabs could be back-hauled from cities which used coal for power generation and the compacted trash would help restore the coal pits. Since a city which uses coal to generate its electricity takes in about the same weight of coal as it produces in solid waste, the compacted waste would be a perfectly balanced back-haul. Our technology and our ecology was thoroughly checked, but in city after city the public service director would finally conclude that he had to struggle along with present makeshift arrangements for reasons of cost—small as these differences are.

But in emphasizing effective demand as the way government persuades the private corporation to participate in defense production or in social problems, I do not want to suggest that exhortation of the managers is unproductive within reasonable limits. President Thornton F. Bradshaw of Atlantic Richfield Company puts it this way in discussing an unsuccessful hard core employment attempt:

> "The effort must be within competitive tolerance. Whereas we can stand a dry hole in Philadelphia on a hard core program, a small company could not stand a single dry hole. And we can't stand ten of those dry holes."

The overall impact is relatively small as we have seen from Figure IV in the second lecture, of persuading management by exhortation to diminish corporate profit. Far better—at a ratio of 10 or 50 or 1,000 to 1 that the firm be persuaded to participate in the process of solving social problems. But management has broad discretion to spend on some probable dry holes if persuaded it makes social sense. For example, the Federal Jobs Program and many others have depended largely on exhortation, and the "E Flag" awards given during World War II and later adapted to the export effort proved to be immensely effective.

Indeed when I see what some of my business friends get talked into and think of some of the things I and my colleagues have been persuaded to do and to give, I wonder if I should stress the limits of exhortation. It is like the Catholic girl who fell in love with a Jewish boy and was told by her parents to exhort him on the advantages of Catholicism with the hope of conversion. When her parents found her weeping a few days later and asked why, she explained that her exhortation had been more effective than anyone expected. Her boyfriend had decided to become a priest. Surprisingly effective as exhortation may sometimes be, tax incentives on the whole will be much more certain. Suppose the Internal Revenue Code was changed so that corporate contributions up to 1% were not deductible at all, from 1% to 3% were deductible at 1½ times the gift, and from 3% to 5% were deductible dollar for dollar. Such a plan might well raise average corporate giving from 1% to 3% and create the equivalent in charitable income of eight more Ford Foundations.

Conservative businessmen along with many radical social critics, however, oppose the delegation to business management of decisions on charitable giving, implementation of low income housing programs, integration of blacks into the work force, and all the other programs which I have suggested would benefit from appropriate use of the powerful thrust toward efficiency and innovation provided by putting firms into competition with each other. The difficulty with these opponents of corporate social responsibility is that they fail to understand how the economic system we have inherited works with the political system we have inherited and how public expectations and economic theory have changed and are changing. To some the issue may seem to be a conflict of fundamental values—a conflict between centralized government control and the personal freedom found in a political economy based on the ideas of John Locke and Adam Smith. But this fails to distinguish between Chamber of Commerce rhetoric and business reality. Our generation no more chose a market economy to make impersonal resource allocation decisions than people in the Middle Ages chose feudalism. We inherited a mixed economy and we hopelessly confuse the issue when we puff up myths of an entirely free enterprise system rather than recognize the mixed economy which has always been guided in some part by public action—land grants to railroads, workmen's compensation laws, anti-trust litigation, and tax incentives for building construction. For almost 200 years the American political system and the American economic system have been changing by incremental steps. There is no reason to believe that new measures of national and corporate performance will not produce another series of incremental changes sufficient to meet our new needs and our new values.

Such optimism is based upon a form of game theory, but not the elegant mathematical game theory of John von Neumann and Oskar Morganstern but the simpler game theory of Knute Rockne and Casey Stengel. It has been my observation that the coaching staff and the team at very few colleges overlap between chess and football—so we also must be specific when we refer to the relevant games. Part of our problem with the traditional economic theory of the firm is that champion chess students are projecting their refined strategies of profit maximization into the skulls of average football players who just want to do better than last year. The theorists are trying to grade alternate management decisions on a scale from zero to one hundred for decision makers who simplify matters to pass-fail grading and who will respond promptly to publicly changed scoreboards and goals. So pretty sloppy quantification will suffice for us to get started on some sort of social accounting. If we have too many dials and they are all calibrated for fine tuning, we really will not be able to learn or to explain much at all. The important thing is to measure roughly the impact of what we are doing, put it on a scoreboard and change our course if necessary. Social change is very slow compared to financial change. Prices and profits must be followed daily, but minority employment, pollution, and our social problems have come gradually into crisis and can be measured with less instant and precise instruments—just as the ship captain for his rough and slow purposes can ignore much of Copernicus and his successors and pretend that the sun and stars go around the earth as Ptolemy believed.

Since the day when the factory owner lived on the hill, managed the plant himself, and really functioned in an Adam Smith economy, the American economy has grown vastly larger and structurally different. Decisions are made by a professional managerial group which is often far removed from the plant and the work force. So long as American society's principal concern was for the growth of total material output at diminishing unit cost, this system with its highly refined financial and cost accounting was sufficient. If we understand clearly how it differs from the world of Adam Smith, how it can be motivated today, where the political problems are, and how public values have changed, we can put together a program of changes that should meet the new necessities. My own program has five points:

A. First of all, we need to reform our Congressional processing of the budget and we need to establish an institution to analyze and publicize the relationship of National Budget decisions to our social problems. To accomplish this I would suggest that Senator Mondale's proposed Council of Social Advisors be integrated with the present Council of Economic Advisors and the Joint Council be required to predict (and support with detailed arguments) both economic cost and social consequences so that the public will appreciate both the dollar and the nondollar trade-offs. For example, the Joint Council might say "We can have 6% unemployment and this will stop inflation, but the black unemployment will be 24% and the white 3%" or "We can cut air pollution from electric generation by 75% but electric bills will go up 20% and no new air conditioning can be installed in any city of 25,000 population or more unless other electric usage is reduced." In addition, the annual budget message of the President would have to be analyzed by the Joint Council of Economic and Social Advisors with a breakdown of how much of our resources are being used to reach socially important goals. We have had distinguished Commissions on National Goals several times but their reports have been diffuse and their impact has been small—in some large part, I think, because they have not been compelled to give quantified judgements on specific social problems such as could be required from the Joint Council. The cost benefit analysis which has been required for some years on waterways improvement projects offers something of a preliminary model of what can be done. The recommendations of such a Council would be in form such that national opinion could be tested by private polling organizations and such that clear political issues on expenditures could be developed in a fashion not possible with our present Congressional piecemeal voting on the budget.

B. The need for such government changes should not cause private business firms to delay in preparing their own sets of social accounts. Initially a firm must make an inventory of what it is doing and not doing on various social problems and then start developing the sets of social accounts that will be necessary. This we have learned in my company is not an easy task even though we limited our first social accounting efforts to minority employment, industrial safety and adequacy of fringe benefits. Executives trained to a scoreboard showing only net income and return on invested capital provide with reluctance figures on minority employment and pollution reduction. They violently object to keeping any statistics which they feel might be misunderstood internally or—worse yet—get out to the public. We found that management people who did not feel their honesty was being challenged by a financial audit would feel that their honesty was being challenged by an attempt to audit their industrial accident statistics. I think this resistance is made up of three elements: (a) normal resistance to anything new, (b) a realization that in the absence of top management monitoring reasonably good results have not been obtained in many of these areas and (c) uneasiness as to how the performance in these areas will be weighted by top management in judging executive performance. For example, one of our executives said to me "I can either hire hard core unemployed or I can maintain the return on equity." He was, in all fairness, not much helped by my reply that he was expected to do both. The thing needed within the company itself is some idea of the extent of the trade-off top management desires to make between socially responsible conduct and maximum net profit. Until we have our books of social account in better order, this is hard for top management to provide. Take, for example, the costs of pollution abatement. If we do not keep careful count of these, we will lose track of what our abatement requirements are doing to our international competitiveness and then be in no position to make policy decisions on the resulting economic problems.

C. An important strengthening of corporate social concern would be the adoption of a sort of anti-trust rule which we might call an anti-lack-of-concern rule which would require divestment of any substantial property or significant operation not visited in person within each 12 months by the executive ultimately responsible for it. An alternative might be to divest the executive. Some might argue that such a rule would reduce the economies of scale or require too much executive travel. It has not really been established that efficiencies of scale are attained by increasing the size of the firm by adding additional plants. Many of the efficiencies come from increasing the size of the individual plant. As for executive travel, there simply is no substitute for careful on-the-scene observation. Coca Cola immediately changed its Florida citrus operations when top management became aware of the conditions—some years after purchasing the property. A good inspector general will always find many things that the reporting system has not disclosed. But the inspector general still makes it possible for the chief executive officer to weight social concerns too lightly. One problem is the complex trade-offs at the margins of two values. For example, we found that relatively small amounts for paint and shrubbery that top management would willingly have spent to be a good neighbor never got spent because the annual budget arranged by necessity of expenditure and return on investment always ran out before these items were reached. The grubby face we therefore presented to our neighbors would not be picked up in the financial reports but only by personal visit. The remedy is to establish a separate category for the non-necessary and non-profit-creating expenditures so that they are expressly considered and weighed on scales of social responsibility.

D. I would also unclog the market and profit mechanism by facilitating the removal of managements which failed to produce good earnings. Creating a greater pressure for profit might seem contradictory to encouraging social responsibility. After all, Professor Galbraith says that when we want to show foreign visitors our most pleasant factories we tour the same plants that the anti-trust division watches as oligopolies. But my own experience has been that lethargic firms with poor management are the least ready to undertake innovative projects that promise either profit to the firm or fulfillment of a community obligation. This is, perhaps, confirmed by a study done by the Harvard Business School which found that companies given to religious and ethnic prejudice were considered to be badly managed generally both by management trainees and by the company executives. Similarly a recent study found that the large paper companies with the worst record for pollution had, generally, the worst profit record. Recent legislation to aid incompetent incumbent management withstand take over tenders violates our whole logic of the free enterprise system.

E.   The pressures placed on management by compelling disclosure of some social indicators is obvious; and as the costs of noncompliance mount, financial auditors may insist that such disclosure has become essential to the accuracy of the traditional financial statements. There is an advantage for socially concerned top management in such disclosure. Not only will it aid internal efforts to create social accounting but it will put pressure on competitors and government to raise the requirements for all. But, once again, it is essential that price tags be put on the social activities so that the macro-information for broad policy decisions can be gathered and so that all concerned can appreciate the trade-offs.

The last four of these five points would make managements more responsive to both market and nonmarket pressures and, at the same time, even better acquainted with their physical properties. They would be made more ready to respond when exhorted to exercise their discretion—in Bradshaw's phrase, to go one more dry hole. The first point, however, is essential for massive social change. We must make it politically possible to allocate to our social problems through government budgets a substantial part of the annual increase in national product.

All of this will be accomplished only after we have better developed both government and business social accounting and have achieved public disclosure and public understanding. Then we should be far better able to measure our problems and to clarify our goals and priorities. This is not the prescription for instant cure. It took a good many years for the cures of Keynes and Kuznets to become acceptable and effective. We must once again develop theory rooted in reality and statistical data which is current and comprehensive. Wonders will not be accomplished overnight and we will have political brawls and errors of decision along the way. Most of us, however, when the fog of Chamber of Commerce rhetoric has cleared have always seen America as an unfinished society—not a *condition* of being a great society, but a *process of becoming* a better society. Not a *situation* to be enjoyed but a *dream* to be accomplished. And when we try in coordination with government policy changes to apply the energies and techniques and incentives of business corporations ever more broadly in the area of our social problems, we must ask critics of industry to be a little patient and to remember the prayer that the late Martin Luther King was fond of quoting from a black Southern minister:

> "Lord, we ain't what we ought to be.
> We ain't what we want to be.
> We ain't what we're going to be.
> But, thank the Lord, we ain't what we was."